What Do You Call a Baby Crab?
And Other Baby Fish and Ocean Creatures

EMMA NATHAN

BLACKBIRCH PRESS, INC.

WOODBRIDGE, CONNECTICUT

Published by Blackbirch Press, Inc.
260 Amity Road
Woodbridge, CT 06525
web site: http://www.blackbirch.com
e-mail: staff@blackbirch.com

© 1999 Blackbirch Press, Inc.
First Edition

Printed in Singapore

10 9 8 7 6 5 4 3 2 1

Photo Credits
Cover: ©P. Parks/OSF/Animals Animals; pages 3, 5, 7, 9, 11, 13, 15, 19: ©Corel Corporation; page 4: ©Breck P. Kent/Animals Animals; page 6: ©Kjell B. Sandved/Photo Researchers; page 8: Allan Power/Photo Researchers; page 10: ©R. Jackman/OSF/Animals Animals; page 12: ©OSF/Animals Animals; page 14: ©P. Parks/OSF/Animals Animals; page 16: ©Jeffery C. Rotham/Peter Arnold; page 17: ©Doug Perrine/Inner Space Visions; page 18: ©Steve Earley/Animals Animals; page 20: ©National Marine Fisheries Service; page 21: ©Schafer & Hill/Peter Arnold; page 22: ©Dan Guravich/Photo Researchers.

Library of Congress Cataloging-in-Publication Data
Nathan, Emma.
    What do you call a baby crab?: and other baby fish and ocean creatures / Emma Nathan.—1st ed.
    p. cm.—(What do you call a baby—)
    Includes bibliographical references.
    Summary: Provides the special names for such baby ocean animals as the fry, shark pup, and spat, describing their physical characteristics and behavior.
    ISBN 1-56711-365-6
    1. Marine animals—Infancy Juvenile literature. [1. Marine animals. 2. Animals—infancy.] I. Title. II. Series: Nathan, Emma. What do you call a baby—
QL122.2.N28 1999   99–20528
591.77—dc21   CIP

Contents

What do you call a baby trout **?**

◆◆ WHAT DO YOU KNOW? ◆◆

Small Frys

To lay her eggs, a female trout will scoop away some gravel on the bottom of a stream, lake, or ocean. Then she will deposit many eggs in the nest she has made. The male will cover the eggs with sand. When they hatch, the fry live in the nest for a while. As they grow, they feed on the yolk sacs from the eggs they were in. When they are big enough to leave their nest, they are called fingerlings. At that point, the young fish start to feed on small ocean creatures.

What do you call a baby crab?

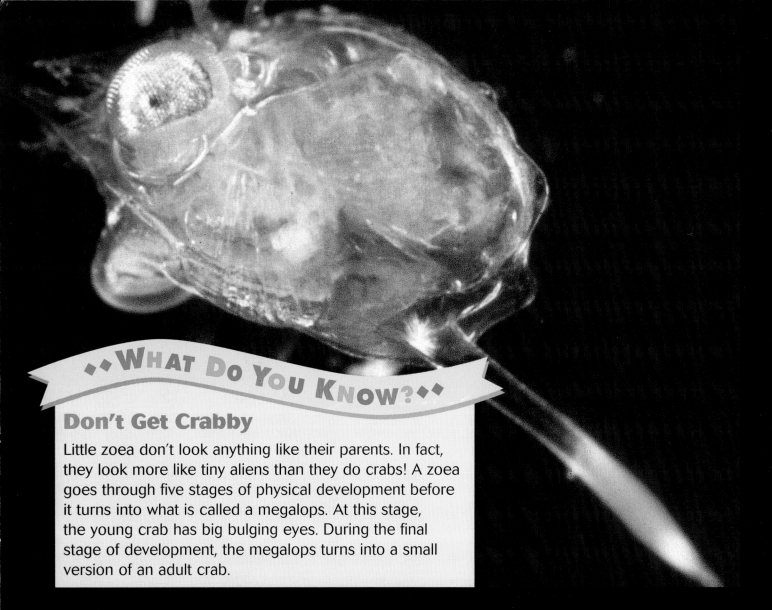

Don't Get Crabby

Little zoea don't look anything like their parents. In fact, they look more like tiny aliens than they do crabs! A zoea goes through five stages of physical development before it turns into what is called a megalops. At this stage, the young crab has big bulging eyes. During the final stage of development, the megalops turns into a small version of an adult crab.

A baby crab is called a zoea or a megalops.

What do you call a baby cod?

Spawn Til Dawn

Cod like to do everything in large numbers. They travel in large schools. And when a female is ready to spawn (lay eggs) she does it in large quantities. In fact, an average female cod will produce 2.7 million eggs in one spawning period! Why so many eggs? It's because most of them get eaten by other fish. To make sure some of her eggs actually become little hakes or sprats, the female lays many more eggs than could ever possibly be fertilized.

What do you call a baby eel?

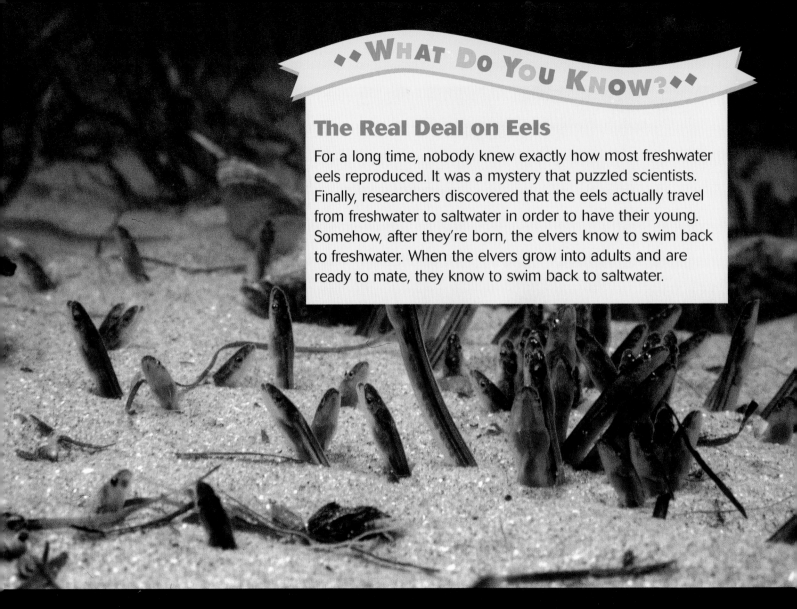

The Real Deal on Eels

For a long time, nobody knew exactly how most freshwater eels reproduced. It was a mystery that puzzled scientists. Finally, researchers discovered that the eels actually travel from freshwater to saltwater in order to have their young. Somehow, after they're born, the elvers know to swim back to freshwater. When the elvers grow into adults and are ready to mate, they know to swim back to saltwater.

A baby eel is called an elver.

What do you call a baby lobster?

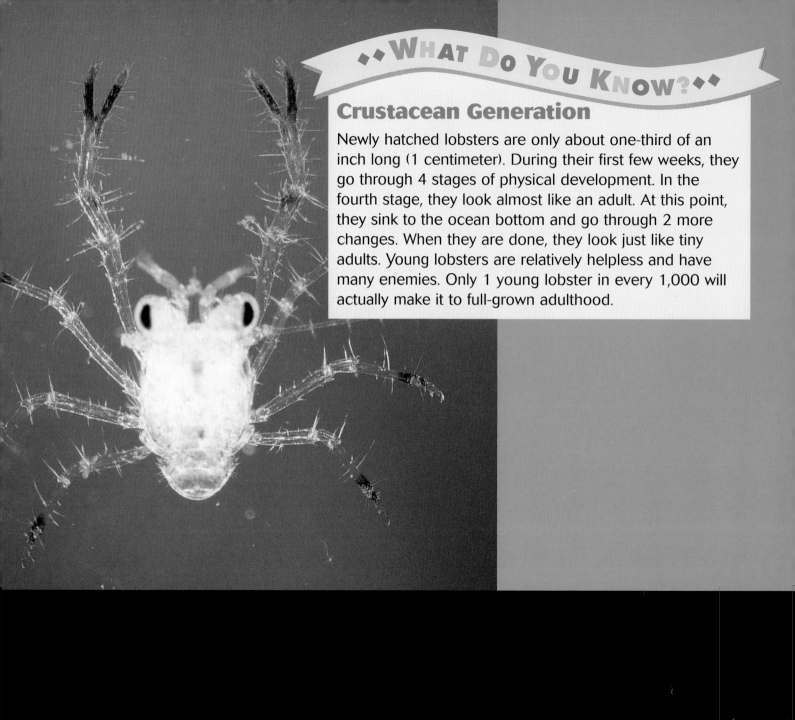

Crustacean Generation

Newly hatched lobsters are only about one-third of an inch long (1 centimeter). During their first few weeks, they go through 4 stages of physical development. In the fourth stage, they look almost like an adult. At this point, they sink to the ocean bottom and go through 2 more changes. When they are done, they look just like tiny adults. Young lobsters are relatively helpless and have many enemies. Only 1 young lobster in every 1,000 will actually make it to full-grown adulthood.

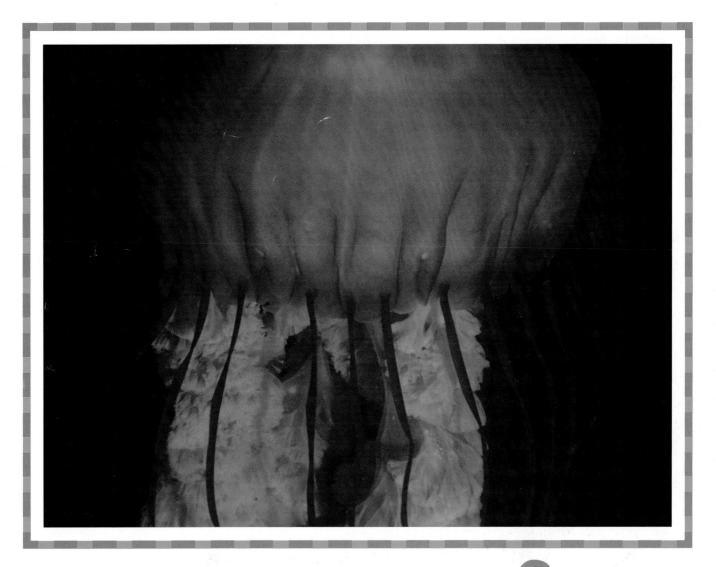

What do you call a baby jellyfish**?**

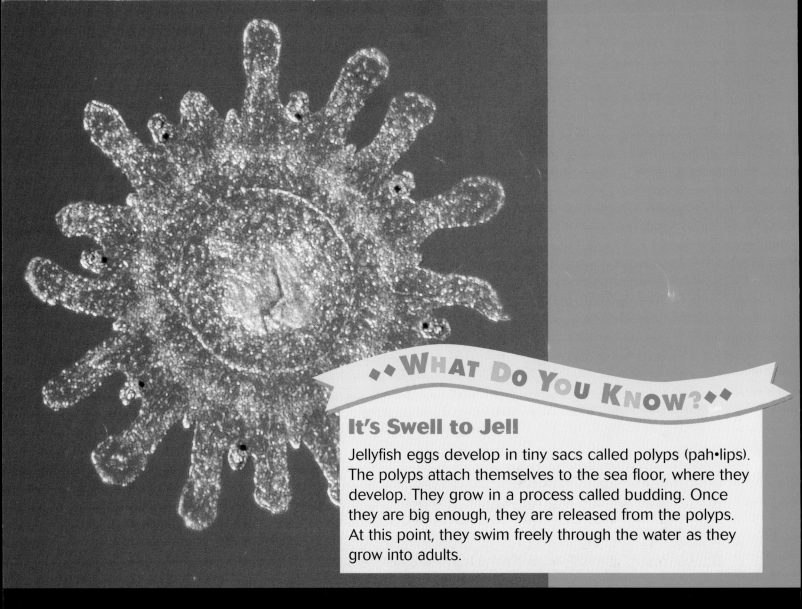

◆◆ WHAT DO YOU KNOW? ◆◆

It's Swell to Jell

Jellyfish eggs develop in tiny sacs called polyps (pah•lips). The polyps attach themselves to the sea floor, where they develop. They grow in a process called budding. Once they are big enough, they are released from the polyps. At this point, they swim freely through the water as they grow into adults.

A baby jellyfish is called an ephyra (eh•fy•rah).

What do you call a baby shark?

Hey Pup, Grow Up!

All sharks develop in eggs. Most shark eggs, however, hatch inside the mother's body. When they do, "live" pups come out. Some smaller sharks (and rays) lay eggs that are covered in a tough, leathery pouch. This pouch is often called a "mermaid's purse." It has long "straps" coming out of its 4 corners. You can often find empty mermaid's purses washed up on the beach.

A baby shark is called a pup.

What do you call a baby mackerel **?**

••WHAT DO YOU KNOW?••

Something's Fishy

A female mackerel can produce up to 500,000 eggs each time she spawns. Each egg contains a drop of oil that helps it float near the water's surface. Many of these eggs can hatch within 96 hours of being laid. Despite the huge numbers, only 1 or 2 of these newly hatched spikes will survive to adulthood. Many that do survive, however, can lead long lives. Some mackerel have been known to live 20 years!

A baby mackerel is called a spike, blinker, or a tinker.

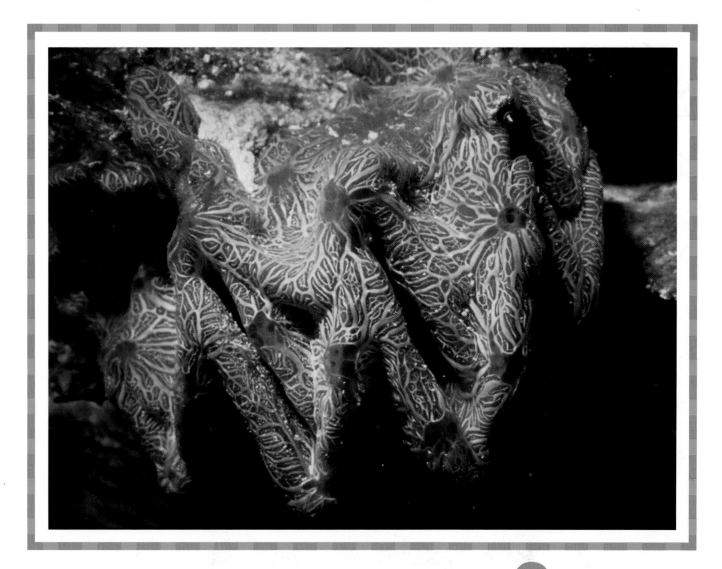

What do you call a baby oyster**?**

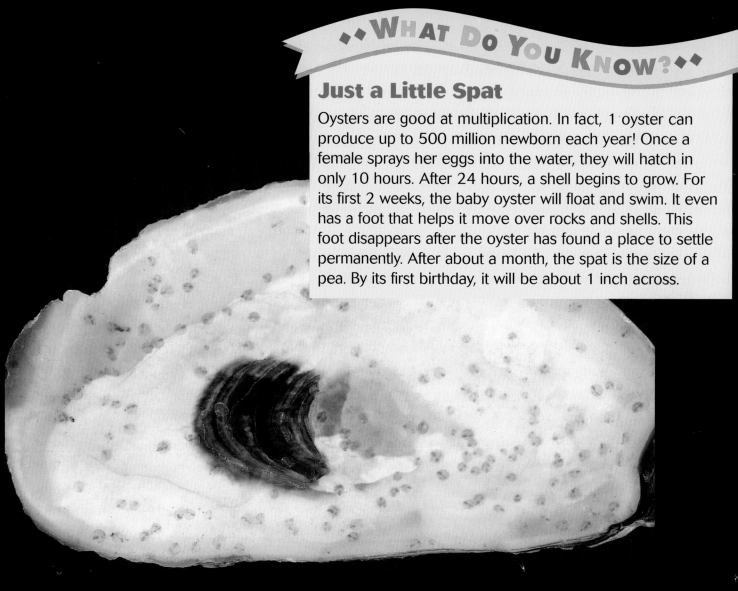

Just a Little Spat

Oysters are good at multiplication. In fact, 1 oyster can produce up to 500 million newborn each year! Once a female sprays her eggs into the water, they will hatch in only 10 hours. After 24 hours, a shell begins to grow. For its first 2 weeks, the baby oyster will float and swim. It even has a foot that helps it move over rocks and shells. This foot disappears after the oyster has found a place to settle permanently. After about a month, the spat is the size of a pea. By its first birthday, it will be about 1 inch across.

A baby oyster is called a spat.

What do you call a baby salmon?

You'll Go Far as a Parr

Most salmon will spend their adult lives in the salty waters of the ocean. But when a female is ready to lay her eggs, she will swim back to the freshwater river or stream in which she was born. When she finds the right place, the female will lay her eggs in a nest called a "redd." Salmon will lay up to 10,000 eggs at one time. Upon hatching, the young salmon live in freshwater for a time. At about 4 inches (10 centimeters) in length, with blotches on its skin, it is called a parr. At about 8 inches (20 centimeters) in length, the parr is called a smolt. Smolts head back to the ocean to begin their lives as adults.

Some Other Baby Ocean Creatures

Megalops	**Larva**	**Sprat**	**Spat**	**Pup**
crab	*lobster*	*cod*	*oyster*	*shark*
lobster	clam	herring	sea snail	ray
	mussel			
	shrimp			

Glossary

Budding—in the early stages of maturity.

Develop—to grow and take on adult characteristics.

Fertilize—the beginning of reproduction when the male's sperm joins with the female's egg.

Fingerling—a small fish up to one year of age.

Fry—a recently hatched or juvenile fish.

Multiplication—increase in numbers, as in reproduction.

Polyp—a protective mass of swollen cells.

Reproduce—when animals mate and produce babies.

School—a group of fish or other sea creatures.

Spawn—a large number of eggs laid by a fish or amphibian.

Yolk sac—the yellow part of an egg. If the egg is fertilized, the protein and fat from the yolk nourishes the developing embryo.

For More Information

Books

Housby, Trevor. *Freshwater Fish* (Concise Collection). New York, NY: Chelsea House, 1997.

Parker, Steve. Dave King (Photographer). Colin Keates (Photographer). *Fish* (Eyewitness Books). New York, NY: Knopf, 1990.

Ricciuti, Edward R. *Fish* (Our Living World). Woodbridge, CT: Blackbirch Press, Inc., 1993.

Rotman, Jeffrey L. (Photographer). Mary M. Cerro. *Lobsters: Gangsters of the Sea.* New York, NY: Cobblehill, 1994.

Snedden, Robert. Adrian Lascom (Illustrator). *What Is A Fish?* San Francisco, CA: Sierra Club Juveniles, 1993.

Web Sites

Marine Biology Learning Center

Find out how fish swim, breathe, reproduce, and relate to their surroundings— www.odysseyexpeditions.org.indexfh.htm

Sharks & Their Relatives

Learn about the physical characteristics, habitat, senses, behavior, and reproduction of these underwater creatures—www.seaworld.org/Sharks/pageone.html

Index